100%
Vegetarian

Snacks under 10 minutes

TARLA DALAL

S&C

SANJAY & CO.
BOMBAY

Second Printing : 2001
Copyright © Sanjay & Co.
ISBN No. 81-86469-53-2

Price : Rs. 190/-

Published & Distributed by :
SANJAY & COMPANY,
353, A-1 Shah & Nahar Industrial Estate,
Dhanraj Mill Compound,
Lower Parel, (W), Mumbai - 400 013. INDIA.
Tel. : (91-22) 496 8068 Fax : (91-22) 496 5876
E-mail : sanjay@tarladalal.com

Recipe Research & Production Design
PINKY DIXIT
ARATI KAMAT
JYOTI JAIN
USHMA NEGANDHI

Photrography
VINAY MAHIDHAR

Food Styling
NITIN TANDON

Designed by
S. KISHOR

Printed by
JUPITER PRINTS,
Mumbai.

OTHER BOOKS BY TARLA DALAL

WESTERN COOKING
The Complete Italian Cook Book
The Chocolate Cook Book
Eggless Desserts
Mocktails & Snacks
Soups & Salads
Mexican Cooking
Easy Gourmet Cooking

HEALTH COOKING
Low Calorie Healthy Cooking
Eat Your Way to Good Health
Pregnancy Cook Book
Baby and Toddler Cook Book

INDIAN COOKING
Tava Cooking
Rotis & Subzis
The Complete Gujarati Cook Book
Desi Khana
Mithai
Chaat
Achaar aur Parathe

EASTERN COOKING
Chinese Cooking
Thai Cooking

GENERAL COOKING
Exciting Vegetarian Cooking
Party Cooking
Microwave Cooking
Quick & Easy Vegetarian Cooking
Saatvik Khana

Pleasures of Vegetarian Cooking
Delights of Vegetarian Cooking
Joys of Vegetarian Cooking
Cooking With Kids
Mixer Cook Book

MINI SERIES
A New World of Idlis & Dosas
Cooking under 10 Minutes
Pizzas and Pasta
Roz Ka Khana
Microwave Desi Khana
T. V. Meals

INTRODUCTION

Faster preparation means more time for recreation. Everyone likes to enjoy an occasional treat during a relaxing moment. Just because such moments are all too few, the ideal snack is one which is quick and easy to prepare while being delicious to eat.

Here is a book dedicated to all my readers who want to make their leisure time more enjoyable. Treat yourself, your family and your friends to a truly unique taste experience in less than ten minutes. With little more than a snap of your fingers, make tasty snacks from this book.

I have divided the book into different sections — Breakfast Delights, Any Time Munchies, Snacky Meals, Cocktail Tit-bits and Cheesy Delights. I have also included some of my favourite sauces and dips in the basic recipe section to accompany the snacks and help you to serve your family and guests better. The easy to follow recipes in each section will help you to plan snacks for any time of the day almost effortlessly.

All the waffle recipes in the book are easy to prepare and the results are always spectacular. For spur of the moment enjoyment, try out the Spiced Sesame Popcorn, a crispy snack relished by everyone. Waffles with Butter and Honey, Moong Dal and Paneer Chila, Chatpata Dahiwala Bread are wonderful recipes for a busy morning. You can bring special flavour to your party with Zucchini and Yellow Pepper Sandwich, Paneer Walnut and Celery Rolls, Spinach Cheese Cigars and Quick Cheese Fondue. If you are looking for a wholesome snack, Vegetable Rice Cake and Hakka Mushrooms with Rice Noodles will leave you completely satiated.

The key to relaxed entertaining is organizing one's work and keeping ingredients handy before cooking. Success is sure to follow. By way of example, for the recipe of Spicy Paneer and Spring Onion Tartlets, the preparation is made easier by using ready-made samosa pattis to make the tarts. Likewise, boiled potatoes, urad dal flour, moong dal flour should be kept ready at all times in the kitchen to help you save a lot of your precious time while cooking.

This book will prove useful to the busy housewife who can not only spend time at work and with her family but also make them happy with very attractive and unusual tasty snacks.

I wish all my readers happy cooking under 10 minutes.

Tarla Dalal

INDEX

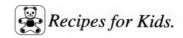

COCKTAIL TIT-BITS

CHEESY DELIGHTS

BASIC RECIPES

BREAKFAST DELIGHTS

SPICED WHOLEMEAL AND OAT PANCAKES

A delightful breakfast recipe combining the goodness of wheat flour and oats with a judicious blend of spices. You have probably never used these ingredients together at the same time but trust me — they make lip smacking pancakes.

● PREP. TIME : 5 MIN. ● COOKING TIME : 8 MIN. ● MAKES 6 PANCAKES.

½ cup whole wheat flour (gehun ka atta)
2 tablespoons quick cooking rolled oats
a pinch nutmeg (jaiphal) powder
a pinch cardamom (elaichi) powder
¼ teaspoon cinnamon (dalchini) powder
1½ tablespoons powdered sugar
2 tablespoons melted butter
¾ cup milk
½ teaspoon Eno's fruit salt

● OTHER INGREDIENTS
butter for cooking

● FOR SERVING
butter and jam

1. Combine all the ingredients except the fruit salt in a bowl.
2. Whisk till it is a smooth batter.
3. Heat a non-stick pan and grease it with butter.
4. Add the fruit salt to the batter and mix well.
5. Pour spoonfuls of the batter on the pan to make 50 mm. (2") diameter pancakes, cooking on both sides (with butter) till golden brown.
   Serve hot with butter and jam or whipped cream and fruits.

✳ Add the fruit salt to the batter just before you are ready to cook the pancakes.

VARIATION
SPICED WHOLEMEAL AND OAT WAFFLES
Use the same recipe to make waffles on a well-greased waffle iron.

MOONG DAL AND PANEER CHILA

Wholesome moong dal pancakes topped with paneer and spices. Moong dal flour used in this recipe is available at provision stores. If not available, substitute it with ½ cup of yellow moong dal (split yellow gram) soaked and finely ground.

● PREP. TIME : 5 MIN. ● COOKING TIME : 8 MIN. ● MAKES 8 CHILAS.

1 cup yellow moong dal (split yellow gram) flour
1 teaspoon ginger-green chilli paste
a pinch asafoetida (hing)
¼ teaspoon sugar
½ teaspoon Eno's fruit salt
salt to taste

● TO BE MIXED INTO A TOPPING
½ cup paneer (cottage cheese), crumbled
2 tablespoons chopped coriander
½ teaspoon chaat masala

● OTHER INGREDIENTS
oil for cooking

1. Combine the moong dal flour, ginger-green chilli paste, asafoetida, sugar and salt and add enough water to make a thick batter. Add the fruit salt and mix gently.
2. Heat a non-stick tava (griddle), pour a ladleful of the batter on the tava and spread it evenly to make a thin pancake (approx. 5" diameter). Sprinkle with a portion of the topping mixture and cook on both sides over a medium flame, using a little oil to cook.
3. Repeat for the remaining batter to make 7 more chilas.
   Serve hot.

CRUNCHY POTATO PANCAKES

A wonderful recipe for a busy morning. Cook these pancakes as soon as you prepare the mixture, to prevent the potatoes from getting discoloured.

To speed up your cooking, cook 3 to 4 pancakes at a time on a large non-stick tava (griddle).

● PREP. TIME : 5 MIN. ● COOKING TIME : 8 MIN. ● MAKES 10 PANCAKES.

½ cup grated potatoes (raw)
3 tablespoons rice flour (chawal ka atta)
2 tablespoons chopped coriander
2 green chillies, finely chopped
1 tablespoon roasted peanuts, crushed
salt to taste

● OTHER INGREDIENTS
oil for cooking

● FOR SERVING
green chutney, page 77

1. Combine all the ingredients with 3 tablespoons of water in a bowl and mix well.
2. Divide the mixture into 10 equal portions.
3. Heat a non-stick tava (griddle) and spread each portion of the mixture on the tava (griddle) using your fingertips into a circle of 75 mm. (3") diameter. Cook on both sides using a little oil until golden brown.
   Serve hot with green chutney.

WAFFLES WITH BUTTER AND HONEY

Picture on page 17

Crisp, hot waffles served with melted butter and honey are always a welcome surprise for breakfast. These waffles taste best when they are freshly prepared and eaten!
Waffles irons come in many shapes and sizes and this batter works well in all of them. The cooking times may vary slightly depending on the type of waffle iron you are using.

● PREP. TIME : 10 MIN. ● COOKING TIME : 6 MIN. ● MAKES 3 WAFFLES.

> 1 cup plain flour (maida)
> ¼ cup cornflour
> ¼ teaspoon baking powder
> 1 teaspoon (5 grams) fresh yeast, crumbled
> 3 teaspoons sugar
> ¼ cup butter, melted
> ¾ cup milk
> a pinch of salt

● OTHER INGREDIENTS
butter for cooking

● FOR SERVING
honey
melted butter

1. Sieve together the flour, cornflour and baking powder in a bowl.
2. Dissolve the yeast in 3 tablespoons of lukewarm water.
3. Add the yeast solution, sugar, melted butter, milk and salt to the flour mixture and whisk well to make a smooth batter. Keep aside for 8 to 10 minutes.
4. Heat a waffle iron and brush it with butter. Pour ⅓ of the prepared batter in the waffle iron and spread evenly. Bake for 2 minutes or until the waffle is golden brown.
5. Repeat for the remaining batter to make 2 more waffles.
   Serve hot with honey and melted butter.

✳ You can use ½ teaspoon of dried yeast, activated in lukewarm water, instead of the fresh yeast for the above recipe.

SEVIYAN UPMA

This recipe is a variation of the popular South Indian Upma using wheat vermicelli instead of semolina. It tastes great with freshly ground coconut chutney.

● PREP. TIME : 7 MIN. ● COOKING TIME : 8 MIN. ● SERVES 4.

2 cups wheat vermicelli (seviyan)
1 teaspoon mustard seeds (rai)
2 teaspoons urad dal (split black lentils)
1 onion, finely chopped
2 green chillies, chopped
½ cup chopped coriander
juice of ½ lemon
3 tablespoons oil
salt to taste

1. Combine the vermicelli, ½ teaspoon of oil and salt with 2 cups of hot water in a bowl. Cover and keep aside for about 5 minutes or till the vermicelli is soft. Drain and keep aside.
2. Heat the remaining oil in a pan and add the mustard seeds and urad dal to it. When the mustard seeds splutter, add the onion and green chillies and sauté till the onion turns translucent.
3. Add the vermicelli, coriander, lemon juice and salt and toss well. Serve hot.

VARIATION
SAVOURY RICE NOODLE UPMA
Use rice noodles instead of wheat vermicelli for the above recipe and garnish it with ¼ cup of grated fresh coconut.

MOONG DAL DHOKLA

This is my favourite recipe for dhoklas but with a new twist, using moong dal flour instead of soaked and ground moong dal. You can substitute it with Bengal gram flour (besan) to make khaman dhoklas.

Add the fruit salt to the dhoklas just before you are ready to steam them.

● PREP. TIME : 5 MIN. ● COOKING TIME : 9 MIN. ● SERVES 4 TO 6.

● FOR THE BATTER
1 cup yellow moong dal (split yellow gram) flour
1½ tablespoons semolina (rawa)
½ teaspoon citric acid crystals (nimbu ka phool)
1 teaspoon green chilli paste
3 teaspoons sugar
¼ teaspoon asafoetida (hing)
1½ teaspoons Eno's fruit salt
salt to taste
oil for greasing

● FOR THE TEMPERING
1 tablespoon oil
½ teaspoon mustard seeds (rai)
½ teaspoon sesame seeds (til)
2 green chillies, finely chopped
a pinch asafoetida (hing)

● FOR THE GARNISH
1 tablespoon chopped coriander

● FOR SERVING
green chutney, page 77

1. Mix together all the ingredients for the batter, except the fruit salt, using enough water to make a thick batter.
2. Add the fruit salt, sprinkle a little water over the fruit salt and mix well.

13

3. When the mixture rises, pour into a greased thali and steam for about 8 minutes.
4. For the tempering, heat the oil in a pan, add the mustard seeds, sesame seeds, green chillies and asafoetida. When the mustard seeds crackle, add 1 tablespoon of water and pour this over the steamed dhoklas.
5. Garnish with the coriander. Cut into pieces and serve with green chutney.

JAGGERY PANCAKES

Delightfully easy but very tasty pancakes. Serve these pancakes straight from the pan onto serving plates.
Green chillies and jaggery give a new spicy sweet taste to this recipe. Add a little flour if you find the pancakes difficult to make.

● PREP. TIME : 5 MIN. ● COOKING TIME : 8 MIN. ● MAKES 8 PANCAKES.

1¼ cups plain flour (maida)
¼ cup curds, beaten
1 teaspoon green chilli paste
¼ cup grated jaggery (gur)
a pinch of salt

● OTHER INGREDIENTS
oil for cooking

1. Mix all the ingredients in a bowl with 1½ cups of water and whisk well to make a thin batter.
2. Heat a 150 mm. (6") diameter non-stick pan and grease it lightly with a little oil.
3. Pour a ladleful of the batter on the pan and spread evenly to get a pancake of 2 mm. thickness.
4. Spread a little oil from the sides and cook the pancake over a medium flame till evenly browned on one side.
5. Repeat with the remaining batter to make 7 more pancakes.
Serve immediately.

CHATPATA DAHIWALA BREAD

Pieces of bread soaked in tangy yoghurt and sautéed with browned onions. A lip smacking breakfast recipe. It's best to use a "day" old bread for this recipe.

● PREP. TIME : 5 MIN. ● COOKING TIME : 9 MIN. ● SERVES 2.

5 bread slices, cut into cubes
½ cup curds
¼ teaspoon turmeric (haldi) powder
½ teaspoon chilli powder
½ teaspoon cumin seeds (jeera)
¼ teaspoon asafoetida (hing)
3 to 4 curry leaves
½ teaspoon grated ginger
1 onion, sliced
2 tablespoons oil
salt to taste

● FOR THE GARNISH
1 tablespoon chopped coriander

1. In a bowl, combine the curds, turmeric powder, chilli powder and salt with 2 tablespoons of water and mix well.
2. Add the cubes of bread and mix well till the bread is coated with the curd mixture.
3. Heat the oil in a non-stick pan and add the cumin seeds.
4. When they crackle, add the asafoetida, curry leaves and ginger and sauté for a few seconds.
5. Add the onion slices and sauté till they are lightly browned.
6. Add the bread mixture and sauté over low heat, stirring occasionally till the bread browns lightly.

Serve hot, garnished with the coriander.

CARROT DOSAS

Soft pancake-like dosas that are made from rice flour and grated carrots.

● PREP. TIME : 5 MIN. ● COOKING TIME : 8 MIN. ● MAKES 8 DOSAS.

1 cup rice flour (chawal ka atta)
½ cup coconut, grated
¾ cup carrot, grated
2 teaspoons sugar
3 green chillies, chopped
4 to 5 tablespoons curds
4 tablespoons melted ghee
salt to taste

● OTHER INGREDIENTS
oil for cooking

● FOR SERVING
green chutney, page 77

1. Combine all the ingredients in a bowl with enough water to make a batter of dropping consistency.
2. Heat a non-stick tava and grease it lightly with some oil.
3. Pour 1 ladle full of the batter on the hot tava and spread it to get a dosa of 125 mm. (5") in diameter and 3 mm. to 4 mm. thickness.
4. Cook on both sides using a little oil, over a slow flame until golden brown in colour.
5. Repeat with the remaining batter to make 7 more dosas.
   Serve hot with green chutney.

Waffles with Butter and Honey, *page 11* ➲

ANY TIME MUNCHIES

◖ Quick Rice Panki, *page 21*

SPICY PANEER STUFFED BREAD ROLLS

A snack prepared in a jiffy for hungry school returned kids. Deep-fried bread rolls stuffed with a spicy spring onion and paneer filling. Serve these rolls hot with hot garlic sauce, page 79

● PREP. TIME : 5 MIN. ● COOKING TIME : 9 MIN. ● MAKES 8 ROLLS.

12 bread slices
½ cup milk (for soaking the bread)

● TO BE MIXED INTO A FILLING
½ cup paneer (cottage cheese), crumbled
¼ cup spring onions (including greens), finely chopped
1 teaspoon green chillies, finely chopped
salt to taste

● OTHER INGREDIENTS
oil for deep frying

1. Remove the crusts of the bread slices. Soak each bread slice in the milk for 2 minutes. Press the bread slice lightly to squeeze out the excess milk.
2. Crumble the bread and mix well to make a soft dough.

HOW TO PROCEED
1. Divide the bread dough into 8 equal portions and shape into even sized rounds.
2. Flatten each bread round to make a circle of 50 mm. (2") diameter and stuff a portion of the filling in the centre of the circle. Bring the ends of the circle together so as to seal the filling inside.
3. Repeat for the remaining bread dough portions and filling to make 7 more rolls.
4. Deep fry in hot oil till golden brown in colour.
5. Drain on absorbent paper.
   Serve hot.

QUICK RICE PANKI

Picture on page 18

Rice flour pancakes steamed in between banana leaves, are a favourite Gujarati snack. Urad dal flour helps to bind the panki batter and make very thin pankis.

Serve the pankis hot from the griddle and let your guests peel off the banana leaves and enjoy the steaming hot pankis with spicy green chutney.

● PREP. TIME : 5 MIN. ● COOKING TIME : 8 MIN. ● MAKES 12 TO 15 PANKIS.

$\frac{1}{3}$ cup rice flour (chawal ka atta)
1 tablespoon urad dal (split black lentils) flour
1 teaspoon curds
2 green chillies, finely chopped
$\frac{1}{2}$ teaspoon cumin seeds (jeera), crushed
1 teaspoon oil
salt to taste

● OTHER INGREDIENTS
3 banana leaves
oil for greasing

● FOR SERVING
melted butter
green chutney, page 77

1. In a bowl, combine the rice flour, urad dal flour, curds, green chillies, cumin seeds, oil and salt and approximately $\frac{1}{2}$ cup of water. Mix well to make a thin batter.
2. Cut the banana leaves into circles using a 75 mm. (3") diameter cookie cutter.
3. Apply a little oil on each banana leaf.
4. Heat a tava (griddle) and arrange half of the banana leaf circles on the tava.
5. Spread 2 teaspoons of the batter on each leaf and sandwich with another greased banana leaf on top.
6. Cook the panki on both sides till light brown spots appear on the banana leaves and the pancake in between peels off the banana leaf easily.
Serve hot with melted butter and green chutney.

✳ If you do not have a cookie cutter for cutting the banana leaves into circles, cut them in squares and proceed as per the recipe.

SPICED SESAME POPCORN

Sesame, cumin and cheese spiked popcorn is a treat at any time of the day. This is a lovely snack to be enjoyed while watching your favourite television programme.

● PREP. TIME : 5 MIN. ● COOKING TIME : 8 MIN. ● SERVES 2 TO 3.

● FOR THE POPCORN
¼ cup maize kernels (popping corn)
1 tablespoon oil

● FOR THE TOPPING
1 tablespoon sesame seeds (til)
½ teaspoon cumin seeds (jeera)
½ teaspoon chilli powder
½ teaspoon salt
2 tablespoons cooking cheese or mozzarella cheese, grated
1 tablespoon oil

FOR THE POPCORN
1. Heat the oil in a deep vessel, add the popping corn and sauté for a few seconds.
2. Cover with a tight lid and cook on a very slow flame, until all the corn has cooked and popped up (approx. 5 to 6 minutes).

HOW TO PROCEED
1. Heat the oil in a pan, add the sesame seeds and cumin seeds. When the seeds crackle, add the chilli powder and salt. Mix well.
2. Add the prepared popcorn.
3. Top with the cheese and mix well.
   Serve immediately.

RICE KHICHU

A rice flour snack flavoured with cumin and spices. Khichu resembles the South Indian upma in texture and is eaten along with oil, generally pickle oil.

I have made small rounds of the khichu in this recipe. You can make this recipe ahead of time and steam the khichu rounds just before serving. Papad khar is a seasoning available at some specialty stores.

● PREP. TIME : 5 MIN. ● COOKING TIME : 8 MIN. ● MAKES 15 PIECES.

½ cup rice flour (chawal ka atta)
½ teaspoon cumin seeds (jeera)
2 to 3 green chillies, finely chopped
¼ teaspoon papad khar
1 tablespoon oil
½ teaspoon salt

● FOR SERVING
oil or green chutney, page 77

1. Combine the cumin seeds, green chillies, oil and salt with 1½ cups of hot water in a non-stick pan. Boil the mixture for 2 to 3 minutes.
2. Add the papad khar and the rice flour and cook on a slow flame (while stirring continuously so that lumps do not form) till the mixture leaves the sides of the pan (approx. 4 to 5 minutes).
3. Divide the mixture into 15 equal portions and shape each portion into an even sized round. Press the centre of each khichu round, using your thumb to make an indentation.
   Serve hot with oil or green chutney.

CORN PANKI

Small corn pancakes, steamed in-between banana leaves. This recipe is devised for people on a diet or for those who have to cut down on fat. Nevertheless, it's extremely good and very tasty.

● PREP. TIME : 5 MIN. ● COOKING TIME : 7 MIN. ● MAKES 16 PANKIS.

2 nos. corncobs, grated
3 tablespoons semolina (rawa)
2 teaspoons chopped coriander
1 teaspoon finely chopped green chillies
1 tablespoon fresh curds
1 teaspoon oil
salt to taste

● OTHER INGREDIENTS
3 bananas leaves
oil for greasing

● FOR SERVING
green chutney, page 77

1. Using a 75 mm. (3") diameter cookie cutter, cut out 32 rounds of the banana leaves. Grease the banana leaf rounds with some oil and keep aside.
2. In a bowl, combine the corn, semolina, coriander, green chillies, curds, oil, salt and $\frac{1}{3}$ cup of water and mix well.
3. Heat a tava (griddle) and place 16 greased banana leaf rounds on it.
4. Pour a spoonful of the corn mixture on each banana leaf round and cover with another greased banana leaf round. Cook on both sides till the banana leaves brown slightly and the pancake in between peels off the banana leaf easily. Serve hot with green chutney.

POHA KHICHU

A simple Gujarati snack made of flaked rice cooked with spices.

Papad khar is a seasoning that is used in the making of papads and traditionally used in khichu. You will find at some specialty stores.

You can even make the khichu ahead of time and steam it for 4 to 5 minutes just before serving.

● PREP. TIME : 5 MIN. ● COOKING TIME : 8 MIN. ● MAKES 12 PIECES.

1 cup poha (flaked rice)
1 teaspoon cumin seeds (jeera), crushed
¼ teaspoon papad khar (optional)
½ teaspoon chilli powder
1 tablespoon chopped coriander
1 teaspoon salt

● FOR THE TEMPERING
¼ teaspoon mustard seeds (rai)
a pinch asafoetida (hing)
¼ teaspoon sesame seeds (til)
1 teaspoon oil

● FOR SERVING
oil
green chutney, page 77

1. Grind the poha to a coarse powder in a blender. The texture should be similar to semolina (rawa).
2. Combine the cumin seeds, papad khar, chilli powder and 1½ cups of hot water in a non-stick pan. Boil for 2 minutes.
3. Add the powdered poha and cook till the mixture leaves the sides of the pan (approx. 4 to 5 minutes) while stirring continuously so that no lumps form. Add the coriander and mix well.
4. Spread the khichu in a 125 mm. (5") diameter greased thali. Smoothen the surface of the poha khichu using the back of a spoon. Cut into diamond shapes.

FOR THE TEMPERING
1. Heat the oil in a pan and add the mustard seeds. When they begin to crackle, add the asafoetida and sesame seeds.
2. Pour the tempering over the khichu.
   Serve hot with oil and green chutney.

PAPAD POHA

Flaked rice and papad sautéed with spices, peanuts and coconut. Use a thin variety of poha commonly known as "nylon poha", to make a crispier snack. This recipe can be stored in an air-tight container for several days. Add the roasted and crushed papad to it just before you are ready to serve. Munch on this low calorie snack at any time of the day.

● PREP. TIME : 5 MIN. ● COOKING TIME : 8 MIN. ● MAKES 1½ CUPS.

1 cup poha (flaked rice)
1 urad dal papad, roasted and crushed
1 tablespoon raw peanuts
1 tablespoon dry coconut (kopra), cut into thin pieces
2 green chillies, slit lengthwise
4 curry leaves
1 tablespoon roasted chana dal (daria)
1 teaspoon powdered sugar
1 tablespoon oil
salt to taste

● FOR THE TEMPERING
1 teaspoon oil
¼ teaspoon mustard seeds (rai)
a pinch asafoetida (hing)
a pinch turmeric (haldi) powder

1. Roast the poha in a pan and stir occasionally till the poha is crisp (approx. 3 to 4 minutes).
2. Heat 1 tablespoon of oil in a pan, add the peanuts and dry coconut and sauté till they turn golden brown.
3. Add the green chillies, curry leaves and chana dal and sauté for a few seconds. Keep aside.

HOW TO PROCEED
1. To prepare the tempering, heat the oil in a pan and add the mustard seeds. When they crackle, add the asafoetida and turmeric powder and stir.
2. Now add the roasted poha, peanuts, dry coconut, green chillies, curry leaves and chana dal and mix well.
3. Add the sugar and salt and mix well.
4. Cool and store in an air-tight container.
5. Add the roasted papad, mix well and serve.

HARIALI SAMOSA

Crisp patti samosas filled with a spicy green peas and french bean mixture. Ready-made samosa pattis which are available at most provision stores will help you to assemble this snack quickly.

● PREP. TIME : 5 MIN. ● COOKING TIME : 9 MIN. ● MAKES 6 SAMOSAS.

6 samosa pattis
2 tablespoons plain flour (maida)

● FOR THE FILLING
½ cup green peas, boiled and crushed
1 cup french beans, finely chopped and boiled
¼ teaspoon ajwain (carom seeds)
2 green chillies, finely chopped
2 teaspoons lemon juice
1 teaspoon sugar
2 tablespoons poha (flaked rice)
1 teaspoon oil
salt to taste

- OTHER INGREDIENTS
  oil for deep frying

- FOR SERVING
  sweet chutney, page 78

FOR THE FILLING

1. Heat the oil in a pan and add the ajwain, green peas, french beans and green chillies and sauté for 2 to 3 minutes.
2. Add the lemon juice, sugar, poha and salt. Mix well and keep aside.

HOW TO PROCEED

1. Mix a thick paste using the plain flour and water. Keep aside.
2. Fold each samosa patti into a cone (as shown in the diagram below) and stuff with the filling.
3. Seal the edges using the flour paste.
4. Repeat with the remaining pattis and filling.
5. Deep fry the samosas in hot oil over a slow flame till golden brown in colour.
6. Drain on absorbent paper.
   Serve hot with sweet chutney.

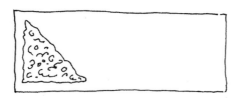
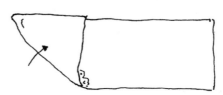

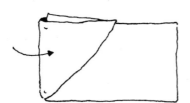

🐻 MOONG DAL KHANDVI

A delicious starter made with yellow moong dal (split yellow gram) flour and curds and tempered with sesame seeds and mustard seeds.

You can even use soaked moong dal instead of moong dal flour for this recipe and follow the same procedure. Soak the moong dal at least 3 to 4 hours before use. A ¼ cup of raw yellow moong dal will yield approximately ½ cup soaked moong dal.

● PREP. TIME : 5 MIN. ● COOKING TIME : 5 MIN. ● SERVES 2.

½ cup yellow moong dal (split yellow gram) flour
½ cup curds
1 teaspoon ginger-green chilli paste
a pinch turmeric (haldi) powder
¼ teaspoon asafoetida (hing)
salt to taste

● OTHER INGREDIENTS
oil for greasing

● FOR THE TEMPERING
1 teaspoon mustard (rai) seeds
1 teaspoon sesame (til) seeds
¼ teaspoon asafoetida (hing)
1 tablespoon oil

● FOR THE GARNISH
2 tablespoons chopped coriander

1. Combine the moong dal flour, curds, ginger-green chilli paste, turmeric powder, asafoetida and salt and ¼ cup of water and mix very well. Heat the mixture in a non-stick pan and cook for 3 to 4 minutes, while stirring continuously. The mixture is ready, when it leaves the sides of the pan.

2. Spread the mixture thinly on the back of three nos. 200 mm. (8") diameter thalis using a flat katori or a palette knife. Allow to cool for five minutes.
3. Smear the khandvi evenly with oil.
4. Cut the khandvi into 50 mm. (2") thick strips. Carefully roll up each strip.

HOW TO PROCEED
1. For the tempering, heat the oil in a pan and add the mustard seeds.
2. When they crackle, add the sesame seeds and asafoetida and pour on top of the prepared khandvis.

    Serve garnished with the coriander.

CRUNCHY BREAD CUTLETS

Crisp, crunchy bread and vegetable cutlets made using a flavourful green coconut paste. Don't make these if you are on a diet – they are so wonderful that it is impossible to stop eating them. You may need to add a little water to the mixture if it becomes too dry and difficult to shape the cutlets.

- PREP. TIME : 9 MIN. • COOKING TIME : 5 MIN. • MAKES 8 CUTLETS.

    5 bread slices
    ½ cup mixed boiled vegetables (carrots, french beans, baby corn), finely chopped
    oil for deep frying

- TO BE GROUND INTO A PASTE
    ¼ cup coconut, grated
    ½ cup chopped coriander
    1 onion, finely chopped
    3 cloves garlic, chopped
    2 green chillies, finely chopped
    salt to taste

- FOR SERVING
    sweet chutney, page 78

1. Grind the bread slices in a blender to make fresh bread crumbs.
2. In a bowl, combine the fresh bread crumbs, vegetables and the prepared paste and mix well to form a soft dough.
3. Divide the mixture into 8 equal portions, shape each portion into even sized rounds and press lightly to make cutlets.
4. Deep fry the cutlets in hot oil over a medium flame till they are golden brown. Drain on absorbent paper.

    Serve hot with sweet chutney.

BAJRA CHAKLIS

Crisp and crumbly bajra and wheat flour savouries flavoured with kalonji. You can deep fry a large batch of the chaklis and store them in an air-tight container. They keep well for several days. Chakli presses are available at utensil stores.

Remember to fry them over a medium flame so that they cook from the insides and they are crisp too.

● PREP. TIME : 9 MIN. ● COOKING TIME : 9 MIN. ● MAKES 15 TO 17 CHAKLIS.

½ cup bajra flour (millet flour)
½ cup whole wheat flour (gehun ka atta)
¼ cup white butter
1 large clove garlic, grated
1 teaspoon kalonji (nigella seeds)
1 to 2 green chillies, finely chopped
1 tablespoon curds
salt to taste

● OTHER INGREDIENTS
oil for deep frying

1. Combine the bajra and wheat flours in a bowl and add the white butter, garlic, kalonji, green chillies and salt.
2. Rub the butter into the flour mixture using your fingertips until the mixture resembles bread crumbs.
3. Add the curds and a little water and knead into a soft dough.
4. Put the mixture into a chakli press and press out round whirls of the dough onto a newspaper or aluminium foil working closely from the centre to the outside of the whirl (approx. 50 mm. (2") diameter). You will get 15 to 17 chaklis.
5. Gently lift each chakli using a flat spoon and deep fry in hot oil over a medium flame till it is golden brown.
6. Drain on absorbent paper.
7. Store in an air-tight container.

✳ You can also bake these in an oven at 180°C (350°F) for 10 minutes on each side. Place them on greaseproof paper, when baking them.

SNACKY MEALS

NACHO STIR-FRY

Picture on facing page

A nutritious blend of ingredients quickly sautéed to make a great accompaniment to tortilla chips. Slightly messy, but fun to eat.

● PREP. TIME : 9 MIN. ● COOKING TIME : 9 MIN. ● SERVES 2.

4 cups tortilla chips (corn chips), page 80

- FOR THE STIR-FRY
  ½ cup onions, sliced
  ½ cup capsicum, chopped
  ½ cup cabbage, thinly sliced
  ¼ cup baked beans (canned)
  1 recipe salsa, see below
  ½ cup grated cheese
  3 to 4 tablespoons milk
  1 tablespoon butter
  salt and pepper to taste

- TO BE MIXED INTO A SALSA
  ½ cup tomato, deseeded and finely chopped
  1 spring onion, finely chopped
  1 large clove garlic, finely chopped
  1 jalapeno pepper (optional), sliced
  1 green chilli, finely chopped
  ½ teaspoon sugar
  ½ teaspoon cumin seeds (jeera) powder
  salt and pepper to taste

- FOR THE GARNISH
  2 spring onions, chopped

Nacho Stir-Fry, *recipe above* ➲

1. Heat the butter and sauté the onions till they are translucent.
2. Add the capsicum and cabbage and sauté for 2 to 3 more minutes.
3. Add the baked beans and salsa and mix well. Cook for 1 to 2 more minutes.
4. Add the cheese, milk, salt and pepper and bring to a boil while stirring continuously.
5. Place the tortilla chips in a large serving bowl and pour the prepared stir-fry over it. Garnish with spring onions and serve immediately.

✳ Tortilla chips (corn chips) are easily available at provision stores. Buy the unflavoured variety, as they are sometimes flavoured with cheese, jalapeno etc.

HAKKA MUSHROOMS WITH RICE NOODLES

Mushrooms stir-fried with rice noodles, spring onions, garlic and soya sauce. Try this oriental stir-fry using baby corn, corn or any other vegetable you like.

● PREP. TIME : 5 MIN. ● COOKING TIME : 9 MIN. ● SERVES 2.

1 cup mushrooms, cut into quarters
1 cup rice noodles
1½ teaspoons chopped garlic
4 spring onions (including greens), chopped
1 tablespoon soya sauce
2 to 3 green chillies, finely chopped
1½ teaspoons cornflour, dissolved in 1 tablespoon cold water
1 teaspoon sugar
2 teaspoons oil
salt to taste

☚ Corn Kebabs, *page 50*

1. Place the noodles in a pan and pour 2 cups of boiling water over them. Cover and keep aside for 5 minutes. Drain and keep aside.
2. Heat the oil in a pan and sauté the garlic and spring onion whites in it. Add the mushrooms and soya sauce and sauté for 2 to 3 minutes.
3. Add the green chillies, cornflour solution, sugar, salt and ¼ cup of water and mix well. Cook for 1 more minute.
4. Add the noodles and spring onion greens and toss lightly.
   Serve hot.

PANEER AND CORN BURGER

This is a perfect no fuss snack for a crowd. Make mini burgers using mini burger buns and make smaller sized patties. A mouthwatering snack.

● PREP. TIME : 5 MIN. ● COOKING TIME : 6 MIN. ● MAKES 4 BURGERS.

4 burger buns
4 tablespoons eggless mayonnaise, page 79
1 tomato, thinly sliced
1 onion, thinly sliced
½ cup shredded lettuce
salt and pepper to taste

● FOR THE FILLING
½ cup paneer, crumbled
½ cup sweet corn (canned), crushed
2 green chillies, finely chopped
2 tablespoons chopped coriander
2 tablespoons bread crumbs
1 tablespoon cornflour
salt to taste

● OTHER INGREDIENTS
bread crumbs for coating
oil for deep frying

- FOR SERVING
  french fries

FOR THE FILLING
1. Combine all the ingredients in a bowl and mix well. Divide into 4 equal portions.
2. Shape each portion into a patty.
3. Coat the patty with bread crumbs.
4. Heat oil in a kadhai and deep fry the patties in hot oil till they are golden brown.
5. Drain on absorbent paper.
   Keep aside.

HOW TO PROCEED
1. Slit each burger bun into 2 halves. Toast both sides of each slit bun lightly on a tava (griddle).
2. Place one patty on the base of a toasted burger bun. Top with 1 tablespoon of mayonnaise, some tomato slices, onion slices, shredded lettuce and sprinkle salt and pepper. Sandwich with the other half of the burger bun.
3. Repeat with the remaining ingredients to make 3 more burgers.
   Serve hot with french fries.

✳ Drain out all the juices of the canned sweet corn before using it for the above recipe.

VEGETABLE RICE CAKE

A nutritious recipe made using instant dhokla mixture and vegetables cooked in a pan.
A quick variation of the traditional Gujarati snack, handvo.

● PREP. TIME : 5 MIN. ● COOKING TIME : 9 MIN. ● MAKES 2 RICE CAKES.

1 packet instant khatta dhokla mix
½ cup grated cabbage
½ cup grated carrot
½ cup grated white pumpkin (lauki)
2 teaspoons ginger-green chilli paste
4 tablespoons chopped coriander
salt to taste

● FOR THE TEMPERING
1 teaspoon cumin seeds (jeera)
1 teaspoon sesame seeds (til)
3 tablespoons oil

● FOR SERVING
green chutney, page 77

1. Squeeze out all the excess liquid from the cabbage, carrot and pumpkin by pressing between your palms. Keep aside.
2. Prepare the dhokla batter following the instructions on the packet.
3. Add the grated vegetables, ginger-green chilli paste, coriander and salt and mix well.
4. Heat half the oil in a 125 mm. (5") diameter non-stick pan, add half of the cumin seeds and sesame seeds. When they crackle, pour half of the batter into the pan.
5. Reduce the flame, cover the pan and allow it to cook for 2 to 3 minutes till the bottom is golden brown.
6. Carefully upturn the rice cake onto the other side and cook for another 4 to 5 minutes.
7. Repeat with the remaining ingredients to make one more vegetable rice cake.

8. Cook both the rice cakes simultaneously on two nos. 125 mm. (5") diameter non-stick pans to speed up cooking.
Serve hot with green chutney.

VARIATION

You can use the same recipe using a packet of instant khaman dhokla mix also.

VEGETABLE QUESIDILLAS

A quick and nutritious version of the famed Mexican starter! Vegetables and cheese make a great filling for these quesidillas.

Ready-made samosa pattis are used in this recipe but you can use tortillas or even left-over chapatis to make this delicious snack.

● PREP. TIME : 5 MIN. ● COOKING TIME : 8 MIN. ● SERVES 4.

10 samosa pattis
butter or oil for cooking

● FOR THE FILLING
½ cup thinly sliced cabbage
½ cup grated carrots
1 medium onion, chopped
2 green chillies, finely chopped
2 cloves garlic, grated
12 mm. (½") piece ginger, grated
¼ cup boiled and mashed potato
½ cup grated cheese
1 tablespoon butter
salt to taste

● FOR SERVING
tomato ketchup or salsa, page 34

FOR THE FILLING

1. Heat the butter in a pan, add the green chillies, garlic and ginger and sauté for 1 minute.
2. Add the cabbage, carrots and onion and sauté for 2 to 3 minutes.
3. Remove from the fire, add the potato and cheese and mix well.
4. Divide the filling into 10 equal portions. Keep aside.

HOW TO PROCEED

1. Spread a portion of the filling on one half of a samosa patti. Fold it into half.
2. Repeat with the remaining samosa pattis and filling.
3. Heat a tava (griddle) and using a little butter, cook the prepared quesidillas on both sides until golden brown in colour.
   Serve hot with tomato ketchup or salsa.

GREEN PEA WAFFLES

A nutritious wholesome snack. Crisp green peas and semolina waffles taste great just by themselves. Urad dal flour used in this recipe is available at provision stores. You can substitute it with rice flour.

- PREP. TIME: 5 MIN. • COOKING TIME : 5 MIN. • MAKES 2 WAFFLES.

1 cup green peas
½ cup semolina (rawa)
⅓ cup urad dal (split black lentils) flour
1 tablespoon curds
3 teaspoons green chillies, finely chopped
1 teaspoon cumin seeds (jeera), crushed
1 tablespoon coriander, finely chopped
¼ teaspoon asafoetida (hing)
½ teaspoon Eno's fruit salt
1 teaspoon oil
salt to taste

- OTHER INGREDIENTS
oil for cooking

1. Grind the green peas in a blender to a coarse paste.
2. Combine the green pea paste, semolina, urad dal flour, curds, green chillies, cumin seeds, coriander, asafoetida, salt, oil and ½ cup of water and make a smooth batter.
3. Add the fruit salt and mix gently.
4. Pre-heat a waffle iron.
5. Lightly grease the waffle iron with some oil, pour half of the green pea batter and spread evenly. Bake for 2 minutes or until the waffle is golden brown.
6. Repeat with the remaining batter.
   Serve hot.

NACHOS WITH GUACAMOLE AND BEANS

A combination of the true Mexican flavours. Guacamole, tortilla chips, beans and cheese make a tasty and exciting snack.

Assemble this recipe just before serving and eat it up quickly!

● PREP. TIME : 9 MIN. ● COOKING TIME : 4 MIN. ● SERVES 2 TO 3.

2 cups tortilla chips (corn chips), page 80
½ cup baked beans (canned)
1 teaspoon chilli sauce
½ cup cooking cheese or mozzarella cheese, grated

● FOR THE GUACAMOLE
½ cup ripe avocado, mashed
1 teaspoon lemon juice
2 teaspoons finely chopped onion
2 tablespoons finely chopped tomato
1 green chilli, finely chopped
salt to taste

FOR THE GUACAMOLE
Mix all the ingredients in a bowl and mash well using a fork. Keep aside.

HOW TO PROCEED
1. In a baking dish, combine the tortilla chips, baked beans, chilli sauce and guacamole and half the cheese and toss lightly.
2. Top with the remaining cheese.
3. Bake in a pre-heated oven at 200°C (400°F) for 3 to 4 minutes or until the cheese has melted.
    Serve immediately.

✳ You can use khakras or papadis instead of tortilla chips for the above recipe.

COCKTAIL TIT-BITS

SPICY BABY CORN FRITTERS

Baby corn pieces dipped in a chilli garlic batter, deep-fried till they are crisp and golden brown.
Make these ahead of time and fry them again when you are ready to serve.
You can fry pieces of cauliflower, broccoli, red, green or yellow capsicum using the same batter. A
great snack for entertaining!

● PREP. TIME : 8 MIN. ● COOKING TIME : 8 MIN. ● SERVES 3 TO 4.

1 cup baby corn, cut into 2 halves vertically
½ cup plain flour (maida)
1 teaspoon cornflour
½ cup buttermilk
1 teaspoon chilli powder
1 teaspoon garlic paste
a pinch soda bi-carb
salt to taste

● OTHER INGREDIENTS
oil for deep frying

● FOR SERVING
hot garlic sauce, page 79

1. Apply salt on the baby corn. Keep aside for 8 minutes. Drain out the excess water.
2. Make a thick batter using the flour, cornflour, buttermilk, chilli powder, garlic paste, soda bi-carb and salt (using a little water if required).
3. Dip the baby corn in this batter and deep fry in hot oil till golden brown in colour.
4. Drain on absorbent paper.
    Serve hot with hot garlic sauce.

BUTTERMILK FRIED ONIONS

Onion rings in a buttermilk batter, deep fried till golden brown. This is a perfect recipe when served with drinks before a meal.

● PREP. TIME : 7 MIN. ● COOKING TIME : 8 MIN. ● SERVES 4 TO 6.

4 onions
1¼ cups plain flour (maida)
1 teaspoon cornflour
1 cup buttermilk
1 teaspoon pepper powder
a pinch of soda bi-carb
salt to taste

● OTHER INGREDIENTS
oil for deep frying

● FOR SERVING
1 teaspoon chaat masala

1. Peel and cut the onions into 12 mm. (½") roundels. Separate the roundels to get onion rings. Keep aside.
2. Combine the flour, cornflour, buttermilk, pepper powder, soda bi-carb and salt and make a batter of pouring consistency using some water.
3. Dip the onion rings in this batter and deep fry in hot oil till golden brown in colour.
4. Drain on absorbent paper.
   Serve hot, sprinkled with the chaat masala.

SATAY STICKS

These skewered vegetable pieces have a superb flavour. Serve these topped or along with the peanut sauce.

● PREP. TIME : 10 MIN. ● COOKING TIME : 8 MIN. ● SERVES 4.

½ cup paneer, cut into 12 mm. (½") cubes
½ cup baby corn, cut into 25 mm. (1") pieces
½ cup green or red capsicum, cut into 12 mm. (½") cubes
1 tablespoon oil

● TO BE MIXED INTO A MARINADE
2 teaspoons curry powder
2 teaspoons lemon juice
2 teaspoons honey
½ teaspoon salt
1 tablespoon oil

● FOR THE PEANUT SAUCE
2 tablespoons peanut butter
½ teaspoon soya sauce
1 teaspoon sugar
½ teaspoon chilli powder
salt to taste

FOR THE PEANUT SAUCE
1. Combine all the ingredients in a pan with ½ cup of water. Mix well.
2. Bring the sauce to a boil. Remove and keep aside.

HOW TO PROCEED
1. In a large bowl, combine the paneer, baby corn, capsicum and the prepared marinade and toss well.
2. Arrange a piece of paneer, capsicum and baby corn on a toothpick. Repeat for the remaining vegetables (to make approximately 15 sticks).
3. Heat the oil on a non-stick tava (griddle) and sauté the satay sticks on all sides till the vegetables brown lightly (approximately 4 to 5 minutes).
   Serve hot with the peanut sauce.

PAPAD PANEER FRITTERS

Chilli-garlic stuffed paneer squares, dipped in batter and coated with coarsely ground papad, deep fried till crisp.

Serve these hot to thoroughly enjoy the contrasting paneer and papad flavours.

A perfect snack for entertaining! Provide wooden or plastic picks to pick up the paneer fritters.

● PREP. TIME : 5 MIN. ● COOKING TIME : 7 MIN. ● MAKES 6 PIECES.

100 grams paneer, cut into 25 mm. (1") cubes
2 tablespoons fresh garlic chutney, page 78
2 papads, raw
¼ cup plain flour (maida)
salt to taste

● OTHER INGREDIENTS
oil for deep frying

1. Slice the paneer cubes into 2 halves. Keep aside.
2. Apply a little garlic chutney on ½ of the paneer cubes. Sandwich with the remaining paneer.
3. Grind the papads in a blender to a powder. Keep aside.
4. Combine the flour with salt and ¼ cup of water to make a thin batter.
5. Coat the sandwiched paneer cubes with the flour batter and then roll them in powdered papad and keep aside.
6. Heat oil in a kadai and deep fry a few paneer pieces at a time, till golden brown in colour.
7. Drain on absorbent paper.
   Serve hot.

CORN KEBABS

Picture on page 36

The addition of rice flour makes these kebabs more crispy and they also absorb lesser oil when deep fried.

You can make these kebabs ahead of time, store them refrigerated and deep fry them just before serving.

● PREP. TIME : 5 MIN. ● COOKING TIME : 5 MIN. ● MAKES 7 KEBABS.

½ cup white corn kernels
¼ cup capsicum, finely chopped
2 green chillies, finely chopped
3 teaspoons rice flour (chawal ka atta)
salt to taste

● OTHER INGREDIENTS
oil for deep frying

● FOR SERVING
green chutney, page 77

1. Purée the corn in a blender, without using any water, to get a coarse paste.
2. Combine the corn, capsicum, green chillies, rice flour and salt and mix well.
3. Divide this mixture into 7 equal portions. Shape each portion into a round, press the rounds lightly to make flat kebabs.
4. Deep fry the kebabs in hot oil till they are golden brown.
5. Drain on absorbent paper.
   Serve hot with green chutney.

PANEER PHUDINA TIKKIS

Serve these crisp mint flavoured paneer tikkis on cocktail plates.
Quite a conversation starter!

● PREP. TIME : 5 MIN. ● COOKING TIME : 5 MIN. ● MAKES 16 TIKKIS.

¾ cup paneer (cottage cheese), grated
4 tablespoons mint, finely chopped
3 green chillies, finely chopped
2 to 3 teaspoons cornflour
salt to taste

● OTHER INGREDIENTS
oil for deep frying

● FOR SERVING
1 teaspoon chaat masala

1. Combine all the ingredients in a bowl and mix well. Divide this mixture into 16 equal portions.
2. Shape each portion into a round and flatten slightly to make tikkis.
3. Deep fry the tikkis in hot oil over a medium flame till they are golden brown.
4. Drain on absorbent paper.
   Serve hot sprinkled with the chaat masala.

PANEER, WALNUT AND CELERY ROLLS

Delicious sandwich rolls stuffed with paneer, celery, walnuts and pieces of crisp iceberg lettuce in a creamy mayonnaise dressing.

For special parties, this combination will be a winner.

● PREP. TIME : 5 MIN. ● COOKING TIME : 4 MIN. ● SERVES 3 TO 4.

4 brown bread slices
½ cup paneer (cottage cheese), cut into small pieces
2 tablespoons celery, finely chopped
2 tablespoons walnuts, finely chopped
2 tablespoons eggless mayonnaise, page 79
2 to 3 iceberg lettuce leaves, torn into small pieces
1 teaspoon oil
salt and pepper to taste

1. Heat the oil in a pan, add the paneer pieces and sauté for 2 minutes. Add salt and pepper and mix well. Keep aside.
2. Remove the crust from the bread slices.
3. Press the slices a little, using a rolling pin. If they crack, steam the slices for 2 minutes and then roll out again.
4. Mix the paneer, celery, walnuts and mayonnaise together. Divide this mixture into 4 parts.
5. Put a portion of the paneer mixture on each bread slice. Top with the lettuce pieces.
6. Roll up tightly and secure the roll by inserting a toothpick. Refrigerate for an hour.

   Serve chilled, cut into pieces.

※ You can make a delicious sandwich using the same filling mixture.

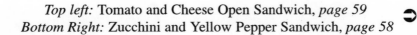

Top left: Tomato and Cheese Open Sandwich, *page 59*
Bottom Right: Zucchini and Yellow Pepper Sandwich, *page 58*

SPICY PANEER AND SPRING ONION TARTLETS

Picture on facing page

Samosa patti tarts filled with a spicy paneer, celery and spring onion mixture.
Your guests will be delighted about the appearance and flavour of the exquisite tarts.
You can vary the filling combination and these tarts will taste just as good.

- PREP. TIME : 5 MIN. ● COOKING TIME : 8 MIN. ● MAKES 6 TARTS.

  - FOR THE TARTS
    2 samosa pattis
    butter for greasing

  - FOR THE SPICY PANEER AND SPRING ONION FILLING
    ½ cup paneer (cottage cheese), cubed
    2 spring onions (including greens), chopped
    2 tablespoons celery, chopped
    1 tablespoon tomato ketchup
    1 tablespoon oil
    salt to taste

  - TO BE GROUND INTO A PASTE
    2 whole red chillies
    2 cloves garlic, chopped
    ¼ teaspoon ginger, grated

FOR THE TARTS
1. Cut each samosa patti into 3 equal parts.
2. Press each samosa patti piece into a greased tart mould (as shown in the diagram below).
3. Arrange the tart moulds on a baking tray. Bake in a pre-heated oven at 200°C (400°F) for 2 to 3 minutes.
4. Store in an air-tight container.

☜ Spicy Paneer and Spring Onion Tartlets, *recipe above*

FOR THE SPICY PANEER AND SPRING ONION FILLING

1. Heat the oil in a pan, add the prepared paste and sauté for a few seconds.
2. Add the paneer, spring onions, celery, tomato ketchup and salt and sauté for 2 minutes.

HOW TO PROCEED

Spoon the hot spicy paneer and spring onion filling into the prepared tart cases. Serve immediately.

STIR AND SERVE MUSHROOMS

Mushrooms stir-fried with onions, tomatoes and oregano to prepare this hot starter almost instantly. Serve this mixture with pieces of pita bread or topped on French bread.

● PREP. TIME : 5 MIN. ● COOKING TIME : 7 MIN. ● SERVES 2 TO 3.

1 onion, sliced
2 cups mushrooms, sliced
1 tomato, sliced
1 teaspoon dried oregano
a dash of tobasco sauce
2 teaspoons oil
salt and pepper to taste

1. Heat the oil in a pan, add the onion and sauté till it turns translucent.
2. Add the mushrooms and some salt and sauté for 3 to 4 minutes.
3. Add the tomato, oregano and pepper and mix well.
4. Finish with the tobasco sauce and serve hot.

CHILLI BEAN DIP

Serve this easy-to-prepare warm dip any season of the year.
For a spicier dip, stir in some chopped green chillies.

● PREP. TIME : 5 MIN. ● COOKING TIME : 7 TO 8 MIN. ● MAKES 1 CUP.

¾ cup baked beans (canned)
¼ cup cheese spread
½ teaspoon cumin seeds (jeera)
½ onion, chopped
1 large clove garlic, chopped
2 spring onions (including greens), finely chopped
1 teaspoon chilli powder
2 tablespoons chopped coriander
1 tablespoon oil
salt to taste

● FOR SERVING
khakras or potato wafers

1. Heat the oil in a pan and add the cumin seeds. When they crackle, add the onion and garlic and sauté for 2 to 3 minutes.
2. Add the spring onions and stir for about 1 minute.
3. Add the baked beans, cheese spread, chilli powder, coriander and salt.
4. Mix well, mashing most of the beans with the back of a spoon till the mixture looks like a thick sauce.
    Serve hot with khakras or potato wafers.

❋ This makes a great sandwich spread too.

ZUCCHINI AND YELLOW PEPPER SANDWICH

Picture on page 53

Grilled zucchini and pepper served topped on crisp chewy French bread slices.

Serve these as a snack or as an accompaniment to soup.

Zucchini or courgette is a variety of marrow (summmer squash). Choose one that has a shiny green outer skin and a firm watery flesh. Zucchini is available at some vegetable vendors and is very seasonal. If zucchini is not available, you can use thinly sliced mushrooms or brinjals.

● PREP. TIME : 5 MIN. ● COOKING TIME : 5 MIN. ● MAKES 6 SANDWICHES.

6 French bread slices
½ zucchini, thinly sliced
½ yellow capsicum
6 to 8 stuffed green olives, sliced
2 teaspoons olive oil or oil
salt to taste

● TO BE MIXED INTO A TOPPING
6 teaspoons eggless mayonnaise, page 79
1 teaspoon finely chopped parsley
freshly ground pepper

1. Heat 1 teaspoon of olive oil in a pan, add the zucchini slices and salt and sauté for 2 minutes. Keep aside.
2. Heat the remaining olive oil in a pan, cook the yellow capsicum, skin side down, until the skin blisters. Cool and peel off the skin. Cut into thick slices. Keep aside.
3. Spread the topping mixture generously on the French bread slices.
4. Top each bread slice with the zucchini and yellow capsicum slices and olives. Spoon a little of the topping mixture over.
   Serve immediately.

✳ Refresh the French bread slices by warming them in a pre-heated oven at 180°C (360°F) for 1 to 2 minutes before you top with the vegetables.

TOMATO AND CHEESE OPEN SANDWICH

Picture on page 53

Cubes of tomato and cottage cheese marinated in herb oil and topped on crusty French bread.
Quick as a wink to prepare! Everyone will enjoy these delicious sandwiches!

- PREP. TIME : 5 MIN. ● COOKING TIME : 2 MIN. ● MAKES 6 SANDWICHES.

    6 French bread slices
    1 teaspoon olive oil or butter

- TO BE MIXED INTO A TOPPING
    ½ cup tomatoes, deseeded and chopped
    ½ cup cottage cheese (paneer), chopped
    2 tablespoons olive oil or oil
    ½ teaspoon dried mixed herbs
    a few fresh basil leaves, chopped
    salt and freshly ground pepper to taste

1. Brush the French bread slices with the olive oil.
2. Bake in a pre-heated oven at 200°C (400°F) for 1 to 2 minutes.
3. Place a portion of the topping mixture on each toasted French bread slice.
   Serve immediately.

PANEER TIKKAS

Cottage cheese and capsicum cubes marinated in tandoori spices.
To get thick curds, hang the curds in a muslin cloth and drain out the liquid. This takes about 15 to
20 minutes. Approximately 1 cup of curds will give you ½ cup of thick curds.

● PREP. TIME : 8 MIN. ● COOKING TIME : 5 MIN. ● SERVES 4.

2 cups paneer (cottage cheese), cut into 50 mm. (2") cubes
½ cup capsicum, cut into 50 mm. (2") pieces
½ cup thick curds
1 teaspoon ginger paste
1 teaspoon garlic paste
2 teaspoons chilli powder
½ teaspoon kasuri methi (dried fenugreek leaves)
½ teaspoon garam masala
2 tablespoons chopped coriander
2 tablespoons oil
salt to taste

● FOR SERVING
1 teaspoon chaat masala

1. Combine the curds, ginger paste, garlic paste, chilli powder, kasuri methi, garam masala, coriander, salt and 1 tablespoon of oil and mix well to prepare a marinade.
2. Add the paneer and capsicum to it and keep aside for 8 to 10 minutes.
3. Arrange the paneer and capsicum pieces on toothpicks.
4. Heat 1 tablespoon of oil on a non-stick tava (griddle) and sauté the paneer tikkas on all sides till they brown lightly (approximately 4 to 5 minutes).
   Serve hot, sprinkled with the chaat masala.

ALOO KURKURE

Poha coated potato and mint croquettes. This couldn't be easier.

- PREP. TIME : 5 MIN. ● COOKING TIME : 8 MIN. ● MAKES 20 PIECES.

1 cup potatoes, boiled and mashed
½ cup mint leaves, chopped
2 to 3 green chillies, finely chopped
1 teaspoon lemon juice
½ teaspoon roasted cumin seed (jeera) powder
salt to taste

- FOR THE COVERING
3 tablespoons plain flour (maida)
⅓ cup poha (flaked rice)

- OTHER INGREDIENTS
oil for deep frying

- FOR SERVING
sweet chutney, page 78

1. Combine the potatoes, mint, green chillies, lemon juice, cumin seed powder and salt and mix well.
2. Divide the mixture into 20 equal portions. Shape into even sized rounds. Keep aside.
3. Combine the flour with a little water to make a thin paste. Keep aside.
4. Grind the poha to a coarse powder in a blender. Keep aside.
5. Dip each potato round in the flour paste and then roll in the powdered poha and coat evenly.
6. Deep fry the potato rounds in hot oil till golden brown.
7. Drain on absorbent paper.
Serve hot with sweet chutney.

SPICY PANEER FRITTERS

Samosa patti coated chilli garlic paneer fritters. You can also use this mixture for a tart filliing.

● PREP. TIME : 5 MIN. ● COOKING TIME : 8 MIN. ● MAKES 16 FRITTERS.

1 cup paneer (cottage cheese), crumbled
1 teaspoon chilli powder
2 large cloves garlic, grated
2 teaspoons tomato ketchup
1 teaspoon cornflour
salt to taste

● FOR THE COVERING
5 tablespoons plain flour (maida)
6 samosa pattis, finely chopped

● OTHER INGREDIENTS
oil for deep frying

● FOR SERVING
green chutney, page 77

1. Combine the paneer, chilli powder, garlic, tomato ketchup, cornflour and salt and mix well.
2. Divide the mixture into 16 equal portions.
3. Shape each portion into a 37 mm. (1½") long cylindrical roll. Keep aside.
4. Make a batter, using plain flour and water.
5. Dip the prepared paneer rolls into the flour batter and then coat them in samosa patti pieces.
6. Deep fry the paneer fritters in hot oil, a few pieces at a time, till they are golden brown in colour.
7. Drain on absorbent paper.
Serve hot with green chutney.

Cheesy Corn Stuffed Jacket Potatoes, *page 72* ➲

CHEESY DELIGHTS

Quick Cheese Fondue, *page 76*

BEAN AND PEPPER TORTILLA PIZZA

A quick pizza that is prepared without using an oven.

Tortillas or chapatis topped with beans, tomatoes, capsicum and cheese. The trick here is to keep the flame sufficiently low while cooking the pizza so that the chapatis or tortillas get crisp and brown but do not burn.

A great idea to use left-over chapatis.

● PREP. TIME : 6 MIN. ● COOKING TIME : 8 MIN. ● MAKES 4 PIZZAS.

4 left-over chapatis or tortillas

● TO BE MIXED INTO A TOPPING
¾ cup baked beans (canned)
½ capsicum, chopped
2 green chillies, finely chopped
¼ cup tomatoes, deseeded and chopped
½ teaspoon chilli flakes
salt to taste

● OTHER INGREDIENTS
1 tablespoon olive oil or oil
½ cup cooking cheese or mozzarella cheese, grated

1. Heat a non-stick pan, add a little olive oil and place one chapati on it.
2. Spoon ¼ of the topping mixture on top of the chapati and sprinkle with some grated cheese.
3. Cover the pan with a lid and cook on a very slow flame till the chapati is crisp and the cheese has melted.
4. Repeat with the remaining ingredients to make 3 more pizzas.
   Serve hot.

CHEESY CORN RAWA WAFFLES

Crispy rawa waffles topped with corn, cheese and tomatoes. A tongue tickling snack. Add the fruit salt just before you are ready to cook the waffles. Eat these waffles as soon as they are made!

● PREP. TIME : 5 MIN. ● COOKING TIME : 8 MIN. ● MAKES 2 WAFFLES.

½ cup semolina (rawa)
⅓ cup urad dal (split black lentil) flour
1 tablespoon curds
1 teaspoon green chillies, finely chopped
½ teaspoon cumin seeds (jeera), crushed
¼ teaspoon asafoetida (hing)
1 tablespoon chopped coriander
½ teaspoon Eno's fruit salt
1 tablespoon oil
salt to taste

● TO BE MIXED INTO A TOPPING
½ cup sweet corn, boiled
½ cup capsicum, finely chopped
2 tomatoes, deseeded and finely chopped
½ cup mozzarella cheese or cooking cheese, grated

● OTHER INGREDIENTS
oil for cooking

1. Combine the semolina, urad dal flour, curds, green chillies, cumin seeds, asafoetida, coriander, oil, salt and approximately 1 cup of water. Mix well to get a smooth batter.
2. Add the fruit salt and mix gently.
3. Pre-heat a waffle iron.
4. Lightly grease the waffle iron with some oil, pour ½ of the waffle batter and spread evenly. Cook for 2 minutes or until the waffle is golden brown.
5. Sprinkle half of the topping mixture on the waffle and warm it up in an open waffle iron for 1 to 2 minutes or until the cheese has melted.
6. Repeat with the remaining batter and ingredients, to make one more waffle. Serve hot.

CHEESE-N-CELERY SANDWICHES

The delightful flavours of cheese, garlic, celery and spring onions combine to make the spread for these sandwiches. This spread is equally good for dainty tea sandwiches or for hearty full-sized sandwiches, too.

● PREP. TIME : 5 MIN. ● NO COOKING. ● MAKES 4 SANDWICHES.

8 bread slices
1 large tomato, thinly sliced
4 lettuce leaves
salt and freshly ground pepper to taste

● TO BE MIXED INTO A SPREAD
½ cup cheese spread
¼ cup eggless mayonnaise, page 79
1 clove garlic, grated
2 tablespoons celery, finely chopped
2 to 3 spring onions (including greens), finely chopped
freshly ground pepper

1. Apply a generous layer of the spread on the bread slices.
2. Place a large lettuce leaf on a slice of bread.
3. Top with the sliced tomatoes.
4. Sprinkle with salt and freshly ground pepper.
5. Sandwich with another slice of bread.
6. Repeat with the remaining bread slices to make 3 more sandwiches.
   Serve immediately.

CHEESY STUFFED POTATOES

In this recipe, the potato is scooped out, stuffed with cottage cheese and celery.
Always keep a few boiled potatoes in your refrigerator to assemble this recipe quickly. Scooped out
potatoes left-over from this recipe can be mashed and used for potato tikkis, a quick sandwich
filling or as a vegetable.

● PREP. TIME : 5 MIN. ● COOKING TIME : 5 MIN. ● SERVES 2.

2 large potatoes, boiled with the skin on
salt to taste

● TO BE MIXED INTO A FILLING
½ cup cottage cheese (paneer), grated
½ cup mozzarella cheese or cooking cheese, grated
2 green chillies, finely chopped
2 tablespoons celery, finely chopped
¼ teaspoon dried mixed herbs
salt to taste

1. Cut each potato horizontally into two halves.
2. Scoop the centres of the potato halves a little, using a spoon so that a slight depression is formed for the filling.
3. Sprinkle the potato halves with salt. Fill the potato halves with the filling mixture.
4. Bake in a pre-heated oven at 200°C (400°F) for 4 to 5 minutes or until the cheese has melted.
   Serve hot.

CRISPY TORTILLA PIZZA

Chapatis or tortillas topped with tomatoes, onions and cheese cooked on a griddle (tava). So quick to make, it is ideal for unexpected guests.

- PREP. TIME : 6 MIN. • COOKING TIME : 8 MIN. • MAKES 4 PIZZAS.

4 left-over chapatis or tortillas

- TO BE MIXED INTO A TOPPING
  ¼ cup finely chopped onion
  ½ cup tomatoes, deseeded and finely chopped
  1 tablespoon chopped coriander
  1 green chilli, finely chopped
  salt to taste

- OTHER INGREDIENTS
  1 tablespoon olive oil or oil
  ½ cup cooking cheese or mozzarella cheese, grated

1. Heat a non-stick pan, add a little olive oil and place a chapati on it.
2. Spoon ¼ of the filling mixture on top of the chapati and sprinkle with some grated cheese.
3. Cover the pan with a lid and cook over a very slow flame till the chapati is crisp and the cheese has melted.
4. Repeat with the remaining ingredients to make 3 more pizzas.
   Serve hot.

MEDITERRANEAN TOASTS

Cherry tomato and mozzarella toasts topped with aromatic fresh basil.
You can lightly toast the hot dog rolls before arranging the topping to make crisper toasts. Use thin tomato slices if cherry tomatoes are not available.

● PREP. TIME : 5 MIN. ● COOKING TIME : 4 MIN. ● MAKES 4 TOASTS.

2 hot dog rolls, slit into two horizontally
10 to 15 cherry tomatoes, cut into 2 halves
½ cup cooking cheese or mozzarella cheese, cut into thin slices
a few basil leaves, torn into pieces
1 tablespoon olive oil or butter
salt and pepper to taste

1. Brush the hot dog rolls with the olive oil. Place the four pieces on a baking tray.
2. Arrange the cheese slices and cherry tomatoes on each hot dog roll half.
3. Sprinkle some salt and pepper and top with basil leaves.
4. Bake in a pre-heated oven at 200°C (400°F) for 3 to 4 minutes or until the cheese has melted.

Serve hot.

CHEESY CORN STUFFED JACKET POTATOES

Picture on page 63

The same topping that goes well with toasted bread goes perfectly with jacket potatoes and makes a lovely tea snack or a delicious supper dish, served along with a soup or a salad.
I assume you will have a few pre-boiled potatoes on hand for this recipe.

● PREP. TIME : 5 MIN. ● COOKING TIME : 8 MIN. ● SERVES 3.

3 large potatoes, boiled with the skin on
salt to taste

● FOR THE FILLING
½ cup sweet corn, boiled
½ cup capsicum, finely chopped
1 tablespoon celery, chopped
2 cloves garlic, finely chopped
1 cup mozzarella cheese or cooking cheese, grated
1 tablespoon cream
1 teaspoon butter
salt and pepper to taste

● FOR THE GARNISH
1 teaspoon chopped parsley
2 to 3 cherry tomatoes, cut into two halves (optional)

FOR THE FILLING
1. Heat the butter in a pan, add the garlic and sauté for a few seconds.
2. Add the sweet corn, capsicum and celery and sauté for a further 2 minutes.
3. Remove from the fire, add the cheese, cream, salt and pepper and mix well. Keep aside.

HOW TO PROCEED
1. Make criss-cross slits on the top of the boiled potatoes.
2. Press the potatoes from the base to open up the slits and to make a cavity for the filling.

3. Sprinkle salt on the potatoes and fill with the filling mixture.
4. Bake in a pre-heated oven at 200°C (400°F) for 4 to 5 minutes or until the cheese has melted.
   Serve hot, garnished with the parsely and cherry tomatoes.

RIVIERA LOAF

This delicious cheese, olive and sun-dried tomato topped bread is perfect with pasta and would also double up as a welcome appetiser!
Cut this loaf into bite size pieces -- perfect for parties, buffets and serving with pre-dinner drinks.

- PREP. TIME : 5 MIN. • COOKING TIME : 5 MIN. • SERVES 4.

   4 hot dog rolls

- TO BE MIXED INTO A TOPPING
   10 nos. sun-dried tomatoes, soaked in warm water and chopped
   1 tablespoon garlic, chopped
   1 tablespoon chilli flakes
   1 cup cooking cheese or mozzarella cheese, grated
   8 nos. black olives, deseeded and sliced
   8 nos. stuffed green olives, sliced
   1 tablespoon olive oil or oil
   salt to taste

1. Cut each hot dog roll lengthwise into two.
2. Divide the topping into 8 equal portions.
3. Spread each portion of the topping on each cut side of the hot dog roll.
4. Bake in a pre-heated oven at 200°C (400°F) for 2 to 3 minutes or until the cheese has just melted.
5. Cut into pieces and serve hot.

※ You will find sun-dried tomatoes available dry or preserved in olive oil at gourmet stores. If you are using sun-dried tomatoes preserved in olive oil, you do not have to soak them in water. Just drain out the excess olive oil.

CORN AND PESTO MINI PIZZAS

A pesto flavoured creamy corn sauce and cheese topped pizza is a great combination. Cocktail or mini pizza bases are readily available in the market.

Pesto is available ready-made in bottles at specialty stores or you can make it easily at home by following this recipe.

Basil is an important flavouring ingredient used in the pesto. Basil is a herb which belongs to the "tulsi" family. Fresh basil leaves are available at a few vegetable vendors. If you can manage to find a good amount of basil, make a larger quantity of pesto and deep freeze it adding a little more olive oil on top to preserve it better.

● PREP. TIME : 5 MIN. ● COOKING TIME : 5 MIN. ● MAKES 24 MINI PIZZAS.

24 mini pizza bases
butter or oil for greasing

● TO BE MIXED INTO A CORN PESTO SAUCE
½ cup cream style corn (canned)
1 recipe pesto, see below
salt to taste

● TO BE GROUND INTO A PESTO
2 tablespoons basil leaves, chopped
4 walnut halves
1 large clove garlic, chopped
2 teaspoons olive oil or oil
salt to taste

● FOR BAKING
½ cup cooking cheese or mozzarella cheese, grated

1. Place the mini pizza bases on a greased baking tray.
2. Spread a teaspoon of the corn pesto sauce on each pizza base.
3. Sprinkle cheese on top of each pizza.
4. Bake in a pre-heated oven at 200°C (400°F) for 4 to 5 minutes or till the cheese has melted.
   Serve hot.

74

SPINACH CHEESE CIGARS

Crunchy samosa patti rolls, filled with a spicy cheese and spinach mixture. Serve these hot to enjoy the taste of the melted mozzarella cheese. Ready-made samosa pattis are available at most provision stores.

● PREP. TIME : 5 MIN. ● COOKING TIME : 8 MIN. ● MAKES 18 PIECES.

> 6 samosa pattis
> 1 tablespoon plain flour (maida) mixed with 1 teaspoon water

● TO BE MIXED INTO A FILLING
¼ cup spinach, blanched and finely chopped
¼ cup mozzarella cheese or cooking cheese, grated
2 green chillies, finely chopped
salt to taste

● FOR SERVING
hot garlic sauce, page 79

1. Cut each samosa patti into 3 to get 75 mm. x 62 mm. (3" x 2½") rectangular pieces. You will get 18 pieces in all.
2. Mix the flour and water to make flour paste. Keep aside.
3. Place a portion of the filling at one corner of the samosa patti piece. Roll it up tightly starting from the end where the filling is placed (as shown in the diagram below) to make a cigar.
4. Seal the edge of the samosa patti piece using a little of the flour paste.
5. Repeat for the remaining pattis and filling.
6. Deep fry the cigars in hot oil till golden brown. Drain on absorbent paper. Serve hot with hot garlic sauce.

❋ Squeeze out all the water from the blanched and chopped spinach to prevent the cigars from becoming soggy.

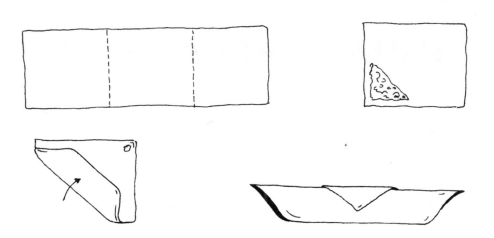

QUICK CHEESE FONDUE

Picture on page 64

Fondue is fun whenever your serve it. Dipping, dunking and then losing morsels of food creates a friendly and informal atmosphere among friends and family.
Cheese spread and milk combine to give a thick, creamy and flavourful fondue almost instantly.

● PREP. TIME : 5 MIN. ● COOKING TIME : 8 MIN. ● SERVES 3 TO 4.

1 cup milk
¾ cup cheese spread
2 tablespoons onion, finely chopped
1 teaspoon cornflour
½ teaspoon chilli powder
1 tablespoon butter
salt to taste

● FOR SERVING
French bread cubes
garlic bread cubes

1. Dissolve the cornflour in 1 tablespoon of cold milk. Keep aside.
2. Heat the butter in a pan, add the onion and sauté for 2 minutes.
3. Add the milk, cheese spread, cornflour solution and salt and mix well.
4. Bring to a boil, while stirring continuously. Sprinkle with chilli powder.
   Serve hot with pieces of French bread or garlic bread.

BASIC RECIPES

GREEN CHUTNEY

A green mint and coriander flavoured chutney which is great for sandwich spreads.
Mint adds freshness to this chutney. The addition of lemon juice enhances the flavours of mint and coriander and prevents discoloration of the greens.
This chutney can be stored refrigerated for upto a week.

● PREP. TIME : 10 MIN. ● NO COOKING. ● MAKES 1 CUP.

2 cups chopped mint leaves
1 cup chopped coriander
1 large onion, sliced
juice of 1 to 2 lemons
1 tablespoon sugar
4 to 6 green chillies
salt to taste

1. Combine all the ingredients and grind to a smooth paste in a blender using very little water.
2. Refrigerate and use as required.

SWEET CHUTNEY

A sweet and tangy Marwari chutney made of dry mango powder, sugar and jaggery with a predominant flavour of dried ginger powder (soonth).

● PREP. TIME : 5 MIN. ● COOKING TIME : 7 MIN. ● MAKES 1½ CUPS.

2 tablespoons amchur (dry mango powder)
½ cup grated jaggery (gur)
½ cup sugar
1 teaspoon chilli powder
½ teaspoon dried ginger powder (soonth)
1 teaspoon fennel seeds (saunf)
½ teaspoon roasted cumin seeds (jeera) powder
salt to taste

1. In a pan, combine the amchur, jaggery and sugar with ¾ cup of water and simmer for 5 to 7 minutes till the sugar has dissolved.
2. Add all the ingredients into the chutney mixture and mix well.
   Use as required. Store refrigerated.

FRESH GARLIC CHUTNEY

The aroma of garlic is unmistakable and pungent. Oil your hands before you peel garlic to prevent your fingers from discolouring and to prevent having a lingering garlic aroma throughout the day! Soaking garlic cloves is hot water makes it easier to peel them.
Make this chutney in large quantities. It stays well refrigerated for upto two weeks.

● PREP. TIME : 5 MIN. ● NO COOKING. ● MAKES ¾ CUP.

1 cup garlic cloves, peeled
1 tablespoon chilli powder
juice of ½ lemon
salt to taste

1. Combine all the ingredients in a blender with ¼ cup of water and grind to a fine paste.
2. Use as required.

HOT GARLIC SAUCE

A spicy dip with a predominant garlic flavour and a dash of tang with the addition of ketchup.

- PREP. TIME : 5 MIN. • COOKING TIME : 2 MIN. • MAKES APPROX. 1 CUP.

¾ cup tomato ketchup
6 whole red chillies
6 large garlic cloves
4 teaspoons oil
a pinch of salt

1. Pound the chillies, garlic and salt in a mortar and pestle to a coarse paste.
2. Heat the oil in a pan till it is very hot. Take it off the flame, add the prepared chilli-garlic paste and stir for 10 to 20 seconds.
3. Add the tomato ketchup and mix well.
4. Cool and use as required.

EGGLESS MAYONNAISE

This is a modified version of the classic mayonnaise sauce, substituting eggs with condensed milk.
You can make larger quantities of this sauce and refrigerate it.
It says well for upto a week when refrigerated.

- PREP. TIME : A FEW MIN. • NO COOKING. • MAKES ABOUT 1 CUP.

½ can (400 grams for full can) condensed milk
4 tablespoons salad oil
4 tablespoons white vinegar or lemon juice
½ teaspoon salt
1 teaspoon mustard powder
½ teaspoon pepper powder

1. Gradually, mix all the ingredients together using a whisk. Store in a refrigerator.
2. Use as required.

※ You can also buy ready-made eggless mayonnaise, which has a longer shelf life.

TORTILLA CHIPS (CORN CHIPS)

Tortillas are the bread of Mexico. Crispy tortilla chips can be used to quickly assemble delicious Mexican snacks. Deep fry a large batch of these chips and store them in an air-tight container. They keep well for several days.

● PREP. TIME : 9 MIN. ● COOKING TIME : 9 MIN. ● MAKES 4 CUPS.

1¼ cups maize flour (makai ka atta)
¾ cup plain flour (maida)
4 teaspoons oil
1½ teaspoons ajwain (carom seeds)
½ teaspoon cumin seeds (jeera)
salt to taste

● OTHER INGREDIENTS
oil for deep frying

1. Mix all the ingredients together and make a dough by adding warm water. Knead very well.
2. Divide the dough into small portions. Roll out each portion thinly with the help of a little flour and prick all over with a fork. Cook lightly on a tava (griddle).
3. Repeat with the rest of the dough.
4. Cut into small triangles and deep fry in oil until crisp.
5. Drain on absorbent paper. Store in an air-tight container.